THE WORLD'S STRANGEST
AUTOMOBILES

THE WORLD'S STRANGEST
AUTOMOBILES

Adrienne Kessel

MetroBooks

This edition published by MetroBooks, an imprint of
Friedman/Fairfax Publishers, by arrangement with
Regency House Publishing Ltd

2001 MetroBooks

M 10 9 8 7 6 5 4 3 2 1

ISBN 1-58663-213-2

3rd printing

Regency House Publishing Ltd
3 Mill Lane,
Broxbourne
Hertfordshire
EN10 7AZ
United Kingdom

Printed in Italy

ACKNOWLEDGEMENTS

*All photographs in this book are supplied by the author, apart from the
following, which were supplied by Andrew Morland:- Pages 11, 47,
60-61, 62 top, 63, 64-65, 78-79 below, 100-101, 102-103, 104-105,
106-107.*

*This book is dedicated to Valerie Ward. Also, special thanks to Geoff
Tuley at the Yorkshire Car Collection, Andy Saunders and Nicola
Chambers.*

*FRONT COVER: The Messerschmitt KR200 with its famous plexi-
glass dome.*
*BACK COVER: The Orange: conceived in the Seventies as part of a
promotional campaign for Outspan oranges.*
*PAGE 2: Despite being a three-wheeler, the Scorpion can match the
stability and performance of many a sportscar. It qualifies as a motorcycle and sidecar combination so it can be driven by anyone holding a
motorbike licence.*
*PAGE 3: This space-age car is based upon a Citroën CX: all body
parts are in steel and were completely redesigned and painted by Andy
Saunders.*
*THESE PAGES: The Velorex was a small car of Czechoslovakian ori-
gin which was produced between 1953 and 1971. It was fitted with a
Jawa two-stroke air-cooled motorcycle engine and had a terrifying top
speed of over 80mph (129km/h). The bodywork was constructed from
wooden panels covered in leathercloth.*

Contents

Introduction

The motor industry itself grew partly from the answers to practical problems, and partly from individual vision. Karl Benz was a draughtsman and designer who started his own business in 1870. His first line of business – building materials – was not providing him with sufficient income, so he turned his attention to engines. The rapidly growing railway system was already revolutionizing the way people worked, the scale on which business was conducted – in short, a whole new way of life was beginning. Benz could see that there was a future for motorized road transport, and he hoped to profit from it.

With some colleagues, Benz started experimenting with gas engines. His first venture was not a success as his partners were less than reliable, but Benz was able to put it all down to experience and start over; he had faith both in his ideas and his ability to put them into practice. By 1883, he had founded a company with two new partners, and his course was set towards the development of the motorized carriage. On 29 January 1886, a patent was issued in Berlin to Karl Benz for his 'vehicle with gas engine drive'. Less than six months later, Benz unveiled his new automobile.

Gottlieb Daimler was driven not so much by practical necessity as by a dream. He was an engineer with experience in the rapidly-expanding locomotive industry, and he believed that it would be quite possible to develop a means of propulsion suitable for, amongst other things, a road-going vehicle. Daimler joined forces with Wilhelm Maybach, and together they worked on the development of the four-stroke engine. He took out a patent on his own engine in 1883. Two years later it was being used to power an early motorcycle, then a boat, and finally in 1886, a carriage.

How strange these early 'motorized carriages' must have seemed. For every enlightened soul who recognized their potential, who appreciated just how much vision, engineering expertise and hard work had gone into their development, there must have been hundreds who laughed, shook their heads and confided to their friends that 'it would never catch on'. Hearing Karl Benz describe how he and his wife listened for hours to the sweet music of his first, workbench-bound engine, many would have thought him crazy – and his wife mad for indulging him. Their opinion of her would have been confirmed had they seen her in 1888 making a pioneering test run of 50 miles (80km) from Mannheim to Pforzheim in her husband's vehicle with her two teenage sons. As usual, a journalist was able to put his finger on the pulse: 'Although the petrol car caused some stir at the Munich Exposition, this employment of the petrol engine will probably be no more promising than the use of the steam engine for road travel.'

RIGHT
Karl Benz was responsible for producing the first automobile in 1886. It was powered by a 924cc engine, which powered the three-wheeled vehicle at speeds of up to 90mph (144km/h).

Chapter One
Back Seat Drivers...

Throughout the latter half of this century there has tended to be a standard and all too readily assumed seating arrangement for the motor car; two in the front, two or three in the rear, all facing forwards. But more recently there has been a move towards freeing the passengers, at least from some of these constraints: people carriers with several rows of seats, estate cars with backward facing rear seats, McClarens where only the driver gets to sit up front, and so on. (Of course, there is safety to be considered: obligatory seat belts all round, babies restrained correctly, dogs harnessed – and there are few sights more anger-inducing than following a car with a 'loose' child on board.)

One thing that modern cars do tend to have in common, though – the driver sits at the front, and faces the direction of travel. Manufacturers have obviously found this a dead-cert winner in the marketing stakes ... but it was not always so. In the early days of motoring there was little need for alarm. Speeds were slow, traffic minimal. Less often than today was a horn used in anger and road rage was best expressed by writing a letter to *The Times* complaining about the potholes in the Bath Road. In those halcyon days, excited and grateful new motorists would celebrate the feat of returning

from Exeter to London with just the one overnight stop (always near Basingstoke); the enlightened would talk of a new age dawning, and the cynics would proclaim the end of civilization as they knew it.

Car manufacturers in those days were naturally unshackled by precedent. There was no mould-breaking to be done – that would have to wait a decade or two. Everything was new. Prior to the success of Messrs. Benz and Daimler, France had been the acknowledged leader in the field of self-propelled road vehicle transport. A number of companies produced steam-powered vehicles, among them De Dion Bouton. But times were moving on, and companies who wanted to stay ahead were going to have to take the new German automobiles very seriously indeed. So De Dion Bouton turned their attention to new technology, and by the turn of the century they were the makers of one of the most popular engines in Europe, a 1.75hp single-cylinder, ideal for motorized tricycles and the like.

De Dion Bouton also produced a best-seller in the shape of its lightweight voiturette. This was powered by a rear-mounted 4.5hp single-cylinder engine, and was the first car to incorporate the now-famous De Dion Tube rear axle. The engine

drove the car through a two-speed gearbox and universally jointed drive shafts. The final drive was not called upon to bear the weight of the car, and the axle could move in relation to the frame without the need for chain drive. The driver sat in comparative comfort towards the back of the car, the controls being located on a vertical pole in front of him. There was room for one passenger to his side, and for a further two in front and facing him. Today's design students looking for something suitably retro should please ignore this one – today's traffic conditions are nowhere near forgiving enough to cope with peering round the passengers.

If the style of the De Dion doesn't take your 1901-fancy, why not try the Sunbeam M/C voiturette of the same

This De Dion Bouton, which is part of the Yorkshire Car Collection, is in near original condition, and still bears the De Dion crest on the sides of the body. It appeared in the film Genevieve.

9

RIGHT
The De Dion's horn looks more like a musical instrument than a car accessory.

year. A British invention this one, although fitted with the De Dion Bouton 275cc single-cylinder engine, giving 2.75hp. The Sunbeam was manufactured by the John Marston tinplate and Japanware company at Ruton on Dunsmore, Staffordshire. The company had been manufacturing bicycles since 1887 and built their first car in 1899, but the voiturette was the first of their models to go into production in a serious way. It was produced until 1904 and sold new at a cost of £130. The wheels are set in diamond formation – one front-centre, one rear-centre, two mid-length. It is allegedly impossible to skid as a result. The driver sat at the rear, the passenger at the front, but both faced out sideways. As well as surely providing good work for osteopaths, since the driver would have had to turn his head sideways most of the time, this seating arrangement has one other great drawback. When turning round corners one way, the passenger tends to get tipped out into the road. And as you may have guessed, turning the other way does the same for the driver – which is disturbing for the passenger's peace of mind, too!

By the time the Victorian era was over and the Edwardian had arrived, motoring was becoming a well-established way of life. It was necessary to be quite well-off to afford to run a motor car, but if money was no object, then with a little help from servants, chauffeur *et al*, it was possible to enjoy hassle-free motoring both at home and abroad. One major advantage of 'abroad' was that Continental roads, especially in France, tended to be long and straight, whereas those in Britain seemed to take detours around every farm, pond

and tree. Consequently, there were more upsets and spills, and the new sensations of speed could not be so readily enjoyed. Once on the open road, however, the true joys of motoring could be indulged.

A popular choice for the upper classes at this time was the Lanchester Open Drive Laundelette. Lanchester started manufacturing cars in Birmingham in 1895, continuing to do so right up until 1956, although in the meantime they were taken over by Daimler and lost a lot of their cachet in the process. The Laundelette was introduced in 1904, and has a vertical 4-cylinder engine giving 20hp positioned between the front seats. As many of these cars were bought by royalty, nobility, maharajahs and so on, they tend to have very ornate coachwork and are highly finished inside and out in expensive, and

BELOW
Not so much a backseat – the whole car is a seat – Minardi Martino's ball car is made from soft foam rubber.

11

LEFT
The Sunbeam is another example from the Yorkshire Car Collection – it is seen here in situ.

usually also immaculate, taste. Interestingly, the speedometer of the Lanchester is placed in the rear of the car; just as he who pays the piper calls the tune, so he who pays the chauffeur determines the speed. Shortage of materials in the immediate post-World War I period had encouraged novel solutions to many practical problems.

Cyclecars – a cross between a cycle and a car – aimed to provide motoring mobility at a more realistic and attainable price than the magnificent but expensive motor cars of the day.

Sabella cars of Mayfair, London, produced cyclecars which they advertised in a particularly English manner:

RIGHT
The front of the Sunbeam, showing the well-respected De Dion Bouton engine.

BELOW
The seats look comfortable enough, but beware the sudden turn to left or right. The odd wheel arrangement may make skidding less likely, but if you don't hold on tight you may be tipped overboard.

TOP
The interior of the Lanchester is luxuriously fitted out in the grand style with quality leather, fine brocade and brass fittings much in evidence.

ABOVE
The speedometer of the Lanchester, positioned in the rear of the car for the convenience of the owner. Chauffeurs must have hated it, dreading impetuous demands to 'speed up' or 'slow down' at impossible moments.

Its unique points may be summarized as follows:
(a) Absolute simplicity of construction.
(b) The upkeep is less than for a tri-car or side-car combination, owing to its flexibility materially reducing the strain on the engine and other working parts, and particularly also the wear and tear of the tyres; whilst the petrol consumption represents only about one gallon to fifty miles running.
(c) No skidding whatever, due to the low centre of gravity and even distribution of weight, the engine being in the front, the driver at the back, and the passenger in the middle, so that whether the passenger is in or not is of no consequence. There is no necessity for non-skid tyres.
(d) There is no differential or gear box.

(e) The car is very light – under 5cwt, and is so low that it is impossible to overturn however fast corners are negotiated.

(f) Every part is of the best material and workmanship, the cars being fitted with the famous J.A.P. twin-cylinder engines, Binks Pilot Jet Carburetters

ABOVE
Motoring from a different era – when class and breeding were all-important. The Lanchester was a car for the well-heeled, *designed to appeal to owner and chauffeur alike. This example is in the Yorkshire Car Collection.*

and 2-inch Michelin tyres.

(g) It is of British manufacture.

Purchasers were pleased with their Sabellas, reporting in glowing terms.

'I have just come back from Eastbourne on my Sabella under the most appalling conditions of mud and rain ... She has covered about 550 miles and not let me down yet, although the roads have been appalling.'

'I am very pleased with the Sabella car. I use the car every day in all weathers, and at weekends my wife and two youngsters make up the load for a jolly tour.'

'I think [the Sabella] is the very best of its kind at present on the market ... I do not think that anyone who has had a ride in one would ever buy a powerful motorcycle and sidecar. The Sabella ... is far ahead of the best sidecar combination made.'

Even journalists could find very little to say that was negative, although Mr Charles F. J. North, signing his article in *Motor Cycling* magazine in 1911 'An untamed amateur', does admit that he owns a Sabella.

'... First let me state that my novitiate in the sport is a thing of the past, and included many a pleasant spin on NSU and Triumph motorbicycles.' Mr North goes on to describe the drawbacks he has found with motorbikes (sideslip, difficulty in giving lifts to a friend), and with sidecar combinations (discomfort of bad road, excessive tyre wear). *'Where lay the solution to my woes?'*, asks the dramatic Mr North. With a Sabella of course!

In France, meanwhile, the cyclecar took on slightly different proportions. The Monotrace was produced between 1925 and 1927, although very few were made, and it is now a very rare collectors' item. This cyclecar is unlike many of its contemporaries in that it has two wheels, not three, but there are two small auxiliary wheels which balance the car when stationary or going very slowly. These are lifted away from the ground when speed is sufficient for balance. The most important thing to remember with the Monotrace is to put the wheels down before stopping, otherwise you fall over sideways! The Monotrace seats two, passenger behind driver, and is powered by a 510cc single-cylinder engine. There is no provision for protection from the elements!

Post-World War II answers to the same problems that the cyclecar was

"Sabella" 1913 Tandem Model.

ABOVE
The Sabella 1913 Tandem model in which the driver sat in the rear.

BELOW
The Sabella Sporting model of 1913 – from the rear. It looks both futuristic and old-fashioned at the same time.

"Sabella" 1913 Sporting Model.

intended to solve saw the scooter come into its own, the new Vespas and Lambrettas bringing low-cost travel to previously untapped markets. But while scooters have gone from strength to strength, the cyclecar was not a huge and lasting success. It did lead on to some interesting developments, however. In 1922 Captain 'Archie' Frazer-Nash and his colleague H.R. Godfrey, who would both go on to build highly successful sports cars, produced the G.N. Vitesse, an air-cooled twin-cylinder with a 1087cc capacity and chain-drive.

Frazer-Nash opened for business under his own banner of A.F.N. Ltd in 1924 in Kingston-upon-Thames, Surrey, later moving a few miles up the road to Isleworth in Middlesex. The 'Chain-Gang Nash' of 1930 got its nickname from the 3-speed crash gearbox which is mounted over the back axle. Having no differential, these cars became popular for grass-

track racing and hill-climbing events: a vintage off-roader.

Fritz Fend was an employee of the Messerschmitt company during the war, and was involved in the development of Germany's first jet aircraft. But once the war was over, he moved out to Roseheim to take over the running of the family business from his father. Travel of various kinds was still very much on his mind, however, and he toyed with the idea of designing and building a completely new form of transport.

At first, Fend worked on a pedal-powered tricycle, for which he designed a unique gearing system. As he had no previous knowledge to work from, and no one else's data to consult, Fend conceived and performed a series of one-man tests. He chose a particular flight of stairs for his experiment, then ran up them carrying various different weights. He repeated the task, ascending one step at a time (low gear)

ABOVE
The Sabella Tandem is fine in this situation though one does worry about what will happen when the little girl grows up – especially if she inherits a penchant for fine and overflowing hats like her mother. Perhaps father has to sit on a cushion.

17

or two or three at a time (higher gear). He recorded his data carefully, and was able to predict how his tricycle might perform. He then produced a working model of the tricycle and was more than happy with the results: but he did begin to realize just how expensive it would be to put his plans into action and his tricycle into production.

However, in 1947, Fend received a visit from a war veteran who had lost both his legs and was anxious to regain some of his lost mobility and independence. Fend reasoned that if the War Wounded Association could be interested in the project, money might be forthcoming to develop it. He produced a prototype vehicle – a small three-wheeled tricycle with a control lever and handlebars. The Association was indeed interested, and it ordered 50 tricycles immediately. They were expensive to make, though, and although Fend recouped his costs he made no real profit from his endeavours. But Fend persevered, building a second version of the tricyle with a covered body. Again the Association was interested, and so this time was the Ministry of Labour in Munich. Fend was at last able to buy proper materials and begin production.

In 1948 Fend bought a power-assisted bicycle, which he intended to use to power his 'Flitzer', as the tricycle had become known. Tests were successful, with the vehicle reaching 25mph (40km/h), but there were obviously a few problems with the suspension and steering. The next test vehicle was fitted with a 100cc Fichel and Sachs engine. This company was very impressed with both Fend and his tricycle and thereafter gave him every assistance they could. The wheels were a problem, too. The bicycle wheels Fend was using were not able to cope with what was required of them but car wheels would have been too large. Fend found the ideal temporary compromise in wheels designed for wheelbarrows. Eventually Fend was able to persuade Dunlop to make tyres for him: by this time he was producing in the region of ten cars per month, the maximum number that he could handle without expanding his business.

Fend looked for a business partner to

BELOW
Body-styling or hair-styling?

RIGHT
Every woman's dream, a convertible with the top down, the wind in her hair...

BELOW RIGHT
...although its a bit of an animal to drive!

help him expand. His first venture in this direction led him close to ruin, for Fend put in all the hard work and long hours, and the partner made most of the money. He then contacted Professor Willi Messerschmitt, with whom he had worked during the war, and who had been most impressed with Fend's ideas and working methods. Messerschmitt was no longer producing aircraft and his company had diversified, but he had plenty of space and facilities available in his factory and was on the lookout for ideas that would maximize potential.

Messerschmitt and Fend set about deciding on the specification of their new product. By 1952, the prototype of the 'Fend Kabinroller' was ready to be tested, with the real thing appearing at the following year's Geneva Motor Show before going on sale to the public. The Fend Kabinroller was a three-wheeled two-seater, the passenger sitting behind the driver. A plexiglass canopy, hinged at one side for access to the cabin, offered weather protection. The engine of the original FK150 was 150cc, with a higher-powered KR175 and KR200 appearing soon after.

Fend decided that it was time to show the world what his little car could do. He prepared a special KR200 for speed record attempts, and in August 1955 it performed a 24-hour test around the Hockenheim circuit. The lap speed average settled to 66 mph (106km/h), and then stayed there for the whole 24 hours. The Messerschmitt broke the record which had been held for seven years by a racing car with much more power, and went on to break at least 25 other land speed records too.

By 1955, the initial teething problems had been sorted out, and the little car was becoming very popular. The interior specification was upped for improved comfort, and a proper suspension was fitted instead of the springs under the seats which had sufficed before. The front track was increased for better stability, changes were made to the

body shape, and the canopy was modified to give a more modern-looking, curved windscreen. Not only the buying public, but also the motoring press found the little Messerschmitt most impressive. One journalist described it as 'The jet for the everyday man – the only car on the market at this price which actually

achieves a perfect harmony between engine and chassis.'

It was around this time that Fend received a communication from Mercedes. They were unhappy that the symbol Fend was using on his car was too similar to their own. Did it really make a difference to a company such as Mercedes? Was the symbol actually that similar anyway? Whatever one might think, Mercedes won the court battle, and Fend had to change his

symbol. He chose three overlapping circles with the initials FMR inset. But Krupps objected to this one, so Fend adopted three diamonds instead. Peace at last!

When the German government began to look once more towards aircraft production, they naturally thought of Messerschmitt. His car-producing division was losing money though, and it was decided that it would have to go. Fend joined forces with businessman Valentine Knott and bought the factory with the intention of going on to produce several different types of vehicle. Fortunately, Messerschmitt kindly allowed Fend to to continue using his name for his creation. The Messerschmitt has an avid following to this day; there are many folk with fond memories of fun days in this vehicle *Messerschmitt*, or being a passenger under the strange little plexiglass dome when they were children.

ABOVE
A rare example of the KR200 convertible. The canopy lifts in the normal way for access. The Messerschmitt shape is very odd, but much loved by its many fans.

Chapter Two
Strange Solutions to Practical Problems

Not all strange cars are created from peculiar ideas or developed from weird afterthoughts. Nor are all born of over-vivid imaginations. Some have started life on the drawing board, as the answer to a practical question, and simply taken a few peculiar turns along the way.

Arnold van der Groot was searching for a good idea. An engineer by trade, he had worked for the Bristol Aircraft Company after the war, and while there had developed an interest in transport generally, and public transport in particular. In 1954 he was studying at university, and needed an engineering-based project to work on. He hit on the

BELOW
The idea of the commuter car has been tried in various countries in Europe – with varying degrees of success. Electric-powered cars are probably the answer for the future as cities are compelled to face increasing traffic problems.

RIGHT
This Shelter is in the process of being renovated. When complete, it will have its skirt-shaped engine cover in place. From the rear, the car then takes on a slightly Dalek-like appearance.

BELOW
With the rear panel removed, access to the engine was easy. The ability to change the engine in five minutes would have been a terrific advantage if the car had succeeded as a city pool car.

ABOVE
The petrol tanks sat under the front seats and were filled through caps in the doors. The other externally recognizable feature of the Sahara is the placement of the spare wheel in a recess on the bonnet lid.

RIGHT
The life of any 2CV tended to be hard – that of the Sahara particularly so. The suspension was set slightly higher than normal to cope with rougher terrain, and there were extra air-intakes above the rear wings.

BELOW
Two of everything – the Sahara has two ignition switches on the dashpanel – one for each engine. There are two choke knobs, too, – situated between the seats. The two engines could be used separately when necessary.

ABOVE
It may have been named after the French
word for 'jewel', but the Bijou, intended to
appeal to the conservative British market,
was never a success. There were several
'made in Britain' choices that were cheaper
– and better.

idea of a pool car for the city – not such a strange idea these days, of course. The convoluted conurbation of Amsterdam was what he had in mind. Small cars would be freely available. They would be hired, driven, and dropped off at the nearest convenient 'car-station'. Design and development

took him almost two years, but he was confident, and the government of the Netherlands was showing an interest in the idea too.

Van der Groot manufactured most of the parts for the car himself, both engine and body. With the exception of some instruments such as the

speedometer, which in truth, but for the legal obligation he need not have bothered about, everything was truly handmade. Most of the body panels were of sheet steel and flat, being rolled into shape where essential. The headlamp surrounds needed to be round – a local saucepan factory was able to supply the demand, presumably without the handles. The engine, which our man also made himself, was a 228cc single-cylinder two-stroke unit producing 8bhp. Its connecting rods were fashioned from standard gas pipe, shaped with a bending machine and welded together – indeed a great deal of Mr van der Groot's 'Shelter' – for that was its name – owed its form to the ancient art of spot welding.

The Shelter's curved roof was formed by a highly ingenious water press. Sheet steel was placed over a pre-shaped concrete mould, and a thick metal plate was clamped on top. Water was then pumped between the sheets of metal, forcing the only thing that would move – the steel – into the shape of the mould. Van der Groot's aim was to produce a small, light, cheap car which was easy to maintain, and in many ways he was on the right track. The Shelter's dimensions are just 6ft 3in (2m) long by 3ft 4ins (1m) wide and 3ft

ABOVE
The driving position inside a Bijou is most peculiar. Unless the driver is very short, eye level is right at the top of the windscreen and visibility can be severely restricted.

BELOW
There was an attempt to echo the styling of the DS in the treatment of the rear of the Bijou. Although the rake of the rear window and the shape of the boot are vaguely familiar, the Bijou has caught none of the DS's style.

LEFT

From a distance, the only clue as to which end of the Janus is the front is given by the wheel arches. When the car is painted all one colour, the ambiguity is even more pronounced.

ABOVE

The engine of the Janus is situated right at the centre. It is accessed through a hatch between the two rows of seats. As the rear seats could be removed, this arrangement is not as inconvenient as it might at first seem.

LEFT

Both front and rear doors of the Janus are large, and hinge out well for access that is really quite good – although it pays not to be too tall. There is storage for small items in functional netting pockets in both doors.

8ins (1.1m) high, and the weight is just 485lb (220kg). Changing the engine took only five minutes with a minimum of effort and manpower. Never mind that the Shelter is so ugly: if the thing had worked and become popular it would have been labelled 'plain-but-functional' or 'crude but practical'. But the Shelter had serious drawbacks of the terminal kind. Axles that snapped like a Twiglet at the first bump in the road, for example – and there are lots of cobbled streets in Amsterdam. Sudden spontaneous combustion too, an instant conflagration with no prior warning – not guaranteed to boast public confidence, or likely to encourage a sale to a government department,

whose interest was definitely not what it was at the drawing-board stage. By the time the curtain finally came down on the Shelter project, van der Groot had enough parts to build 20 cars, but only seven were ever completed. Was his Shelter, although a failure in practical terms, a success as a university project? We may never know!

There are many people who would hold that the Citroën 2CV is a very strange motor car. No one who has witnessed it in its natural habitat, clinging at a precariously alarming angle to the outer edges of French mountain roads, and laden with fruit, bread, wine, chickens, people and so on, could fail to be impressed by its eccentricity. When the Michelin company bought out the Société André Citroën in 1935, it was a matter of great urgency to get the ailing firm back onto its feet as quickly as possible. Michelin had only agreed to buy it because it was the principal creditor, and could see a chance of recouping some of the money it was owed over a period of time. Under the management of Pierre Michelin and Pierre Boulanger, an extremely hard-working and talented organizer who had met Michelin during the war, the company was to be revitalized. A major part of the plan was to be the production of a small car, suitable for the working Frenchman: thus the original design brief specified the need to carry two farmers, dressed ready for work, along with either 110lb (50kg) of potatoes or a small barrel of wine.

To make sure that he was thinking along the right lines, Boulanger sent one of his associates, Jacques Duclos,

on a fact-finding mission around the country. He was to talk to potential customers, finding out exactly what they wanted from their transport, and what their priorities were. Such organized market research was very unusual at that time, but it bore fruit because the results convinced Boulanger that the TPV (*toute petite voiture*) project could be successful. The realization of Boulanger's dream, the 2CV, was introduced at the Paris Salon de l'Automobile in October 1948, and continued in production for over 40 years.

In 1957, Jacques Duclos hit the road again, this time to check out some information that had reached the company through some of its dealers; was there a market for a four-wheel-drive version of the 2CV for use in more extreme conditions? Motoring costs with the 2CV were quite low – it had been designed to go on and on without too much attention, and it was cooled by air which, as the promotional literature pointed out, was always available for free in unlimited quantity. The car should also be able to cope with freezing conditions and tropical ones with equal alacrity. Four prototype 'Saharas' were built and presented to the press in 1958 at a military testing ground quite close to Paris, with the car becoming commercially available two years later. The problems associated with making a car like the 2CV into a four-wheel-drive were solved in a very clever way. The car had two engines, one placed conventionally at the front, the other where the boot would have been, the boot cover being replaced by a panel with integral air-intakes. There were two gearboxes, operated by a single gear-lever, although the rear unit could be disconnected and the car driven in standard mode. In the event of front-engine failure, the rear unit could be used alone.

A second engine in the boot caused

logistical problems, the solutions to which altered the overall design of the car somewhat. As there was no room for the spare wheel in the rear, a special bonnet was designed with a recess to hold it – giving a 'rough terrain' look in passing. Two petrol tanks sat under the front seats, their filler caps set into the doors – not a very safe arrangement by today's standards but there were no reports of conflagrations. There were extra air-intakes above the rear wings, which were cut away, and the suspension was set slightly higher than on a normal 2CV to make travel over rough ground easier.

The Saharas were popular within the rather limited market that they were aimed at. The Spanish police bought 80 on the strength of the car's test performance over sand-dunes, and numbers were sold in North Africa and Switzerland, where they saw service as snow-ploughs. In all, though, less than 700 Saharas were made, with very few surviving today.

The 2CV was of course vastly popular in France, and built up a decent following quite quickly in Holland, Belgium and elsewhere. But in Britain, it never really got off the ground. Of course, there was a limited following from avid Francophiles for whom the car's very Frenchness was a recommendation, and those with the type of broad vision that accepts such things for what they are and celebrates them – perfect or not. But for the majority of the U.K. market the 2CV was just too unrefined, too unconventional, too emotively French. The car was produced at Citroën's own factory in Slough until 1959, at which point it became clear that it was not going to sell in sufficient numbers to make production worthwhile. But a new car, designed specifically with the U.K. market and U.K. foibles in mind was planned and put into production in its place – the Bijou. The Bijou was aimed at a growing sector of the market

– for use as a second car. So the Bijou was an attempt at a conventional-looking saloon car – a shopping car with a boot. Introduced at the Motor Show in October 1959, the Bijou was bodied in glass fibre, and was designed by Peter Kirwan-Taylor, who also styled the Lotus Elite. Some of the styling elements of the Bijou, especially at the rear, reflect those of the Citroën DS, which was quite popular in the U.K. at the time. Some of the parts actually came courtesy of the DS, probably for economic reasons. The Bijou had two doors with very little space in the rear for passengers, and although generally speaking it was not uncomfortable, tall drivers would have had their visibility restricted by the top of the windscreen. The fuel

LEFT
The Kettenrad (literally chain-wheel) is sometimes referred to in full as the Kettenkraftrad (chain-working wheel). Sticklers for precision would prefer to address it as SDKsZ II.

ABOVE
The Kettenrad came in different versions for different applications. This is the smallest, with a towing capacity of half a tonne. It was extremely reliable, but was built on quite a small scale.

BELOW
The motorcycle pedigree of the Kettenrad is easy to see, although parts had to be specially made that would be equal to the arduous tasks for which the vehicle was designed.

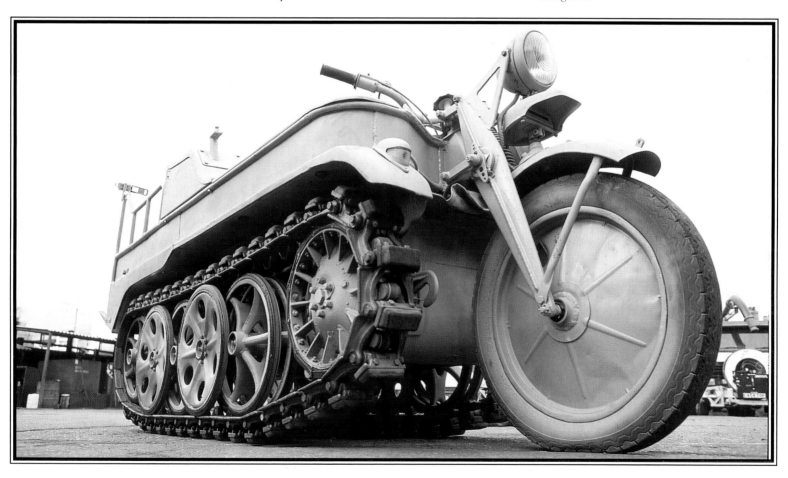

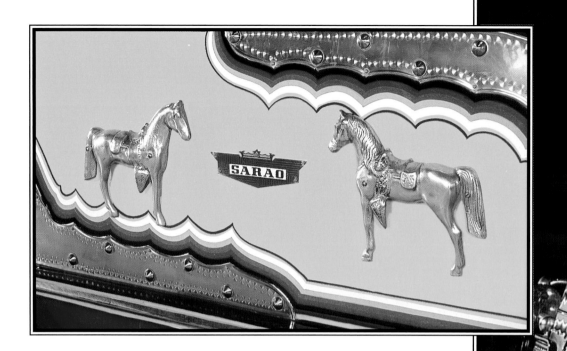

ABOVE

Somewhere on almost every Jeepney is a reference to horses, either painted, in relief, or as statues. They look back to the pre-war era when public travel was by horse and carriage.

BELOW

The horses are beautifully crafted. It is amazing to think that such a culture should have grown out of the devastation of a city through the personal enterprise of two ordinary people.

Jeepney colour schemes are loud, but the graphics are so well done that the effect is warm and cheerful rather than garish. The blaring music systems are as loud as the paintwork – you can't miss hearing or seeing the bus.

consumption was quite good, but unfortunately the car was more expensive than either the Morris Minor or the Mini, both of which had the advantage of being British born and bred. The Bijou fared no better in the sales stakes than the original 2CV, and production ended in 1964 with only 250 ever having been made. Of these only 50 or so survive to the present day.

It is not at all unusual to discover that a manufacturer of motor cars began in business making motorbikes. The necessary practicality and paramount importance of sound engineering that motorbike design demands have helped to keep the designers' eye on the job in hand and their designs unsullied by some of the worst excesses of the stylists' art.

Zundapp was already in the position of being one of the top German motorbike manufacturers by 1955 when it took over the rights to produce the Dornier Delta. Claudius Dornier's symmetrical little car, which appeared at the Frankfurt Motor Show in 1955, was almost triangular viewed from the side, and had two doors, one at each end, both of them hinged at the top. Two people got in at each end, the two rows sitting back to back. Less than four-up, you had to ensure one person was in the driver's seat.

Zundapp modified the original idea of the Delta, producing prototypes of the new Janus by 1956 and going into production the following year. The Janus was named after the Roman god of doorways who was blessed with two opposite-facing heads. He was one of

ABOVE
The exotic and quirky interior of the Jeepney, full of vibrant colour, ornate decoration and loud music!

RIGHT
The driver's compartment is a little less embellished.

the first of the new breed of deities, immortals, muses, etc, commandeered to lend their names to various parts of the calendar, motor cars, confectionery and so on in the name of publicity.

The Janus was more rounded than its predecessor, with deeper arches over the front wheels breaking the symmetry slightly. There was still a door at each end, but now hinged more conventionally at the side. A strange arrangement, the inside of the Janus, but a designed strangeness. The car took four still, or the second seat could be removed for load-carrying. An alarming early press photograph of the car shows it loaded up with a full-size refrigerator. Alternatively, the seats could be converted into a bed for two above the mid-mounted horizontal single-cylinder 248cc engine, with space under each end of the bed for the luggage: only people of smallish dimensions need apply though, the Janus interior is not large, although its overall length is 9.4ft (2.86m) head to head.

Sadly for the little Janus, by the time Zundapp was geared up for full-scale production, other small cars, especially the Isetta, had the market pretty well covered. The Isetta was both quicker, and also very much cheaper than the Janus, and perhaps had more instant 'showroom appeal', too. Zundapp had intended to produce 15,000 per year, but in truth they sold under 7,000 over the first two years. The Janus was going to lose money and so Zundapp reluctantly but sensibly ceased car production and went back to relying on motorbikes. There is a postscript to the Janus story; when the Zundapp factory was shut down in the 1980s, a 'new' Janus was discovered tucked away in a forgotten corner. This car now has pride of place in a Berlin motor museum. So, despite its short production life, the Janus can afford to laugh on the other side of its other face.

So it was the German motorcycle industry of the Fifties that gave us the sweet and friendly little Janus. Two decades earlier, the same industry had been engaged in a rather different, and much less pleasant business, but one of the vehicles it produced was no less strange.

Germany was busy re-arming itself during the Thirties – which meant

Need some extra room in your motorhome? Do what you would do at home – get an extension. The sight of this van in the rear view mirror could give you quite a shock though!

business opportunities for any company in the right line of business. As well as armaments and fighting vehicles, there were a multitude of other supplies to be considered, and one of the many urgent priorities was for a reliable vehicle for towing purposes. The NSU motorcycle company was approached for its ideas. It originally came up with a vehicle that used standard motorbike components, but rigorous testing proved that it was not going to be up to the job, so a redesign was called for, using specially engineered parts and in some cases beefed-up versions of motorcycle ones. By 1940, the first batch of 500 of these vehicles – called the Kettenrad – were ready for use. They came in different versions for specific applications, with towing capacities of half, one, three or five tonnes. The smallest was used for transporting ammunition, or could tow an anti-tank gun. The Kettenrad was extremely popular with the troops who needed to use it. It was rugged and reliable, and it did the job for which it was intended – by no means as much of a foregone conclusion as one might suppose, in any army at any time. It could cope admirably with the mud that dominated the Russian front, and with snow, but also with the hot, dusty sands of North Africa. The Kettenrad was powered by the 1500cc unit designed for the Opel Olympia, with a gearbox specially designed for the job. The top speed was an impressive 50mph (80km), and amazing torque gave the Kettenrad the ability to pull smoothly at as little as 1mph (1.6km/h).

NSU continued to produce the Kettenrad until 1944, with Stoewer also making them for a while. By then, 8345

units had been made altogether. As so often happened at the end of the war, left-over parts were not wasted or destroyed but were maximized for non-combative uses. It is not known exactly how many Kettenrads were assembled under the Allies, possibly a few hundred. They and any surviving earlier examples were put to use as agricultural vehicles – a purpose for which they were excellently suited.

If the post-war devastation of cities across Europe was bad, the situation in Manila in the Philippines was even worse. The city was the second most badly affected in the world, the basic infrastructure of the place decimated, with no public transport of any kind left. As so often happens in such times of crisis, it is not the benevolence and farsightedness of governments and authorities that gets the ball rolling, but

the enterprise and enthusiasm of a handful of individuals. And once again 'left-overs' were the means to an end. One thing that Manila did have was old American army Jeeps. Two enterprising young lads decided to see what they could do with them. They bought a couple, extended the chassis, built people-carrying bodies by hand – and provided some light-relief decoration, too. Suddenly, Manila had a public

transport system again, one with a unique style too!

Today Manila boasts at least 30,000 of these Jeepneys. Nowadays they are powered by Japanese 2300cc Isuzu engines, but the chassis is still handmade, as is the body, all the fittings, and the fantastic decoration. The Jeepneys ply a predetermined route which is written along the side of the vehicle, but there are no bus stops –

people get on and off anywhere and everywhere, simply attracting the driver's attention is enough. You can hear when a Jeepney is coming before you see it, too, as they are all fitted with music systems played loudly. The decoration is always flamboyant and often incorporates one or more horses, a nostalgic look-back to the days before the war when public transport was by a horse-drawn carriage called the Calessa.

Chapter Three
Going to Extremes

Whichever path of life you choose to travel, you will find someone who travelled it faster than anyone else. Or slower. Or was the first person to hop the whole distance backwards. They will tell you all about it in the pub. They may even have witnesses, or a certificate to prove it. The biggest, the highest, the smallest, the tallest, they're all there. And motor cars are no exception.

The Mini is a common enough sight,

RIGHT Would you have expected the inside of Claustrophobia to look boring or ordinary? Straight gear-lever? Circular steering wheel?

BELOW LEFT Claustrophobia's engine protrudes through a cut-out in what might normally be called an engine cover. The car is now part of the Yorkshire Car Collection.

BELOW Claustrophobia – the lowest car in the world according to the Guinness Book of Records of 1988. The car is 14in (36cm) lower than standard, with only a 6-inch slit of windscreen to squint through.

ABOVE
When is a Beetle not a Beetle? When it's Outrage 3, the improbable car created by Brian Burrows for an all-out attack on the Modified Class title of the VW Drag Racing Championships.

BELOW
There is almost nothing of the standard Beetle underneath, though. The Autocraft engine produces 850bhp from its 2.8 litres, running on methanol and nitrous oxide.

taken for granted, part of the British heritage, a member of the establishment. But when it first appeared on the scene in 1959, it was anything but ordinary. After the terrible experiences of the war years, the Fifties were a time of peace and recovery. But they were austere years too, with rationing still in force for some products, and many families having to pick up the pieces of their old lives or rebuild new ones. There were new crises too – the Suez blockade, bringing

a possibly indefinite oil shortage, and new rationing – of petrol this time – as a result. Motorists throughout Europe were looking towards the smaller car – less heavy on fuel, cheaper to buy, run and maintain and manufacturers were looking to supplying the need. In 1957, BMC decided that the time was right for a new small car to hit the market, and gave the job of designing it to Alec Issigonis.

The basic concept of the car was that it would have to carry four adults and

As a long-time Beetle enthusiast, Brian was determined when he built the first version of Outrage that his racer would actually look like a Beetle, and had the fibreglass shell specially made in Florida. For Outrage 3, the bodyshell is moulded in carbon fibre, which saved 250lb (113kg) in weight, but cost £5,000 in money on materials alone. And although it looks like a Beetle, the whole body can in fact be lifted off in one piece!

their luggage. One of the major problems that Issigonis faced was that of the engine. He had been instructed to keep costs to a minimum by using an already-existing BMC power unit which cut the choice down somewhat. He eventually solved the problem by using a modified version of the engine from the A33. His great inspiration was to place the gearbox under the crankshaft instead of behind it; this way the whole unit could be mounted transversely, which shortened the necessary overall length of the car drastically.

The first Minis were produced at BMC's Longbridge works on 4 April 1959, and by August the same year, the car was ready for its full-scale public launch. Unlike many designers in a similar position, Issigonis had no interest in 'style'. He saw himself as an engineer rather than an artist or craftsman, and insisted that his creations were first and foremost practical propositions.

'Practical' is not the first word that springs to mind on first sight of 'Claustrophobia'. Built by Andy Saunders of Poole in Dorset, it featured in the Guinness Book of Records in 1988 as the lowest car in the world. (He does have the certificate to prove it!)

The car has effectively had over 14 inches removed from its height. The windscreen is only six inches deep, and it has been suggested by people who have tried to perfect the technique – their reasons are their own – that one should roll into a ball, and then lie on the floor to drive. Fortunately there is a sunroof, and driving is certainly easier, if somewhat boringly conventional, with the top half of one's body sticking through it. The engine is a 1300cc A series bored out, with twin SU

Carburettors which share the driver's problem – they stick out of the top of their allotted space. The sills come courtesy of a Triumph Herald, the rear lights have a scrapped Allegro to thank, and the hubcaps are plastic aerosol caps. The bright purple car is decorated with 27 hours-worth of graphics, while the inside is suitably unrestrained eyestrain – purple and white stripes all round, with a giant white pretzel for a steering wheel.

The Lincoln company was founded in 1917 by Henry Leland. Rather than name his company after himself, he chose instead the name of the president he had admired so much in his youth – Abraham Lincoln. The company did well, but the cars lacked a certain style. By the time this was rectified, the Depression was upon it, and to make matters worse, it was landed with a hugely excessive tax bill by the U.S. Government. This was in fact a clerical error, which was subsequently corrected, but it had a devastating effect

ABOVE
The lengths some people will go to – a 12-door sedan Ford Lincoln. To buy and run such a car needs serious money. If you're already an oil-baron, however, getting hold of enough petrol won't be too much of a problem.

49

on the business, which was forced into receivership. Lincoln was bought by the Ford Motor Company and soon parted company with the original owner Leland and his family.

After the war was over, General Motors instigated several new marketing ploys to help it stay on top in what it knew would become an extremely competitive marketplace. One of these ploys was the introduction of 'Motoramas', a kind of extravagant theatrical production featuring its cars, and ideal showcases for new and futuristic ideas and concepts. The Motoramas ran from 1949 until 1963, and star of the 1953 show was the new Cadillac Eldorado. One of its most striking and innovative features was the wrap-around windscreen, a device straight out of the aircraft cockpit, but adapted for the motor car.

In 1965, Elvis Presley ordered his very own Cadillac Eldorado Convertible, which was customized for him by Jay Ohrberg. The car was fitted out, as might be expected, in flamboyant style, with gold fittings and a luxurious interior. Presley was not always happy with his motor car though – he once shot it when it broke down, and it eventually fell from favour altogether.

Jay Ohrberg kept the car and wanted to restore it, but the Los Angeles earthquake brought down the roof of

LEFT

This car has survived being shot at by Elvis, the Los Angeles earthquake, raiding by memorabilia hunters and the loss of some of its parts, but it is in the process of being restored to its former over-the-top glory.

ABOVE

The interior of Elvis's Cadillac is a matter of taste.

LEFT

Real gold is not the first choice of material that springs to mind when thinking about those little car parts – surrounds to the windscreen wiper arm, for example – unless of course money is no object.

The DeLorean's body was made entirely from brushed stainless steel and styled by Giugiaro. It was certainly a fine-looking car, although maybe it looked more like a styling exercise than a serious production possibility.

The DeLorean, despite its creator's expectations, never became a star. Even so, the car has its enthusiasts.

BELOW RIGHT
The car's huge gullwings were nothing if not impressive, giving film star-style access to the luxurious interior, which was another of the car's plus-points

his workshop onto the car. Yet it survived, to to be bought by the Yorkshire Car Collection and flown to England. Various parts, including all the fittings and fixtures had been boxed and stored for some years, so restoring the car was always going to be a bit of a jigsaw puzzle. In the event, not all the parts arrived in England. Some 'disappeared' – Elvis memorabilia collectors with no shame are probably to blame – and others may have gone missing just because they were gold and worth money. Some parts did arrive that were absolutely nothing to do with the car though! So the Cadillac is a long-term restoration; some parts may turn up, others will have to be substituted with authentic, period replacements.

There are some cars that have had money lavished upon them – obscene amounts of money in some cases – and there are other cars that come onto the market and sell for a high price just because of their previous owners. Sometimes of course, the two combine. Anything that has an Elvis connection is blessed with saleability.

Not all the cars that have money poured into them result from owner-foibles, though. In the mid-Seventies, John DeLorean developed a car which he intended putting into production in his factory in Ireland. The car made its Motor Show debut in London in 1981. The car with its huge gull-wings was styled by Giugiaro, the body being made entirely of brushed stainless steel. The engine is a 2.8-litre V6, mid-mounted, and is the result of a joint Renault/Peugeot/Volvo exercise. The car was horrendously expensive to build; the commercial implications of this, and the decisions that were made as a result, ran DeLorean into all kinds of trouble, fiscal and legal. Although very much a car that symbolized the

ABOVE
The beautiful motif that adorned the front
of Hispano-Suiza motor cars was designed
by François Bazin. It made its first
appearance at the Paris Salon in 1919, a
special occasion, as it marked the unveiling
of Europe's first post-war motor cars.

BELOW
In the 1920s, the Hispano-Suiza was
one of the most expensive cars of its
class, but popular with those for whom
money was not a major problem.

early Eighties, the DeLorean still has its
fans. Despite its history and
impracticality, it is still an appealing
luxury car with 'love it or hate it' style.

The Hispano-Suiza company was
founded in 1904. It marked the entry of
Spain into the automobile industry,
and founded an automobile line that
would continue until World War II.
France and Germany were already well-
established in the field; an *Autocar*
survey in 1906 published the names of
108 motor car manufacturers, but so far
no Spanish manufacturer had made the
list. The guiding light of Hispano-Suiza
was Marc Bikigt, a designer of
innovation and vision. As early as
1907, his chassis used unit

construction for engine and gearbox – an idea way ahead of its time. In 1911, Hispano-Suiza took over an old tram depot in Levallois, Paris – and became a French concern as well as a Spanish one. The cars were record-breaking in the price department; at the Paris Salon of 1921, the Hispano-Suiza shared with three other manufacturers the plaudit of 'most expensive available' at 90,000 French francs – chassis only of course. The company continued making high-quality automobiles right up to World War II, when it concentrated on the

manufacture of aero engines. At the Geneva Motor Show of 1946, an entirely new V8 Hispano-Suiza engine was unveiled. But it was felt unsuitable to try to introduce high-quality motor cars to Europe in these years of austerity, and the project was shelved.

In the mid-Fifties, Enrico Piaggio decided to manufacture a small car – a proper car – but built on a small scale. His Vespa scooter was already a success and Piaggio believed there would be a good market – those who would like a Vespa but really needed a

ABOVE
Given a different set of circumstances, the little Vespa 400 could have become very popular – perhaps as popular as the Fiat 500. Unlike bubble cars, the Vespa is built like an ordinary car, but on a small scale.

BELOW
The Vespa's interior – plain and functional but well-styled and inviting.

car. His designer Corradino D'Ascanio got to work, and the Vespa 400 was presented to the world at the Paris Motor Show in October 1957.

There was no reason why the Vespa 400 should not have been as successful as the scooter, but Piaggio had reckoned without Fiat. Fiat exerted great influence over the automotive industry in Italy as it was the major supplier of raw materials. Fiat had just announced the 500, and was displeased that it might have a rival, so it put pressure on Piaggio not to make the

ABOVE

ABOVE
Particularly popular in its native Italy,
the APE has found favour in other
European countries, too. This example
makes and sells fresh doughnuts by the
river Thames near Windsor Castle ...

Vespa 400 in Italy. Piaggio agreed to
build the car only in France at the
ACMA factory at Fourchambault, and
the cars would be badged ACMA.

The Vespa 400 was a normal car in
most respects, but scaled down in size.
There was enough room for two
average-sized adults. The doors hinged
at the rear, and this combined with
very generous seat adjustment made
getting in and out really quite
straightforward. A cushion was

available for the rear luggage shelf,
making a seat for two children. The
interior was functional and practical,
with hard-wearing seats and a plain
uncluttered dashboard.

The Vespa 400 engine was an air-
cooled twin-cylinder two-stroke unit of
393cc, giving 14hp and capable of
amazing torque; it could accelerate
away from 25km/h in top gear. The
car's top speed and cruising speed were
both quoted as 55mph (90km/h),

ABOVE RIGHT
... *this one takes visitors on a guided tour around Strasbourg ...*

RIGHT
... *and this one sells ice creams in Amsterdam!*

although it was noisy at this speed. It was very frugal with fuel too. Vespa 400 production began in 1957 and lasted for four years, during which time over 30,000 cars rolled off the production line. Most of the Vespa 400s were sold in France, or the near export market, in particular Belgium and the Netherlands.

There should have been a good market in Europe for a car like the Vespa 400. It cost 20 per cent less than most of the available competition, with all the advantages of compact size, frugality and reliability. It was neither crude, nor uncomfortable. Had the car been able to find its footing in Italy, just like the scooter, things might have been very different.

The first version of APE (APE = bee, just as Vespa = wasp) was introduced in 1948. At the front end it was identical to the Vespa scooter while the rear came in three basic shapes – a flat-bed truck, box van and rickshaw-style carrier for two passengers. But throughout its life, the APE has been converted to suit the owner's business. The APE rider sat on a saddle over the engine, a 125cc unit, with four forward gears, but no reverse. An add-on windshield was available as an extra, and Piaggio introduced a small cab with open sides for the delivery versions, which afforded some protection from the weather.

The APE has been regularly altered and updated throughout its life. The current range has over 50 different variations, including diesel and electric-powered models. In all, more than 1.5 million APEs have been manufactured since this 'working Vespa' was introduced.

Clive Sinclair was an entrepreneurial electronics supremo. He gave us the pocket-sized calculator and helped advance the cause of personal computing in ways which today we take for granted. In the early Eighties, Sinclair had the idea of building a

vehicle which would solve road congestion, pollution and fuel waste at a stroke. He believed it would be the ultimate city vehicle, ideal for business people, ideal as a second family vehicle. Of course, he also believed that it could be a commercial success and was therefore prepared to finance the project out of his own pocket.

In theory, the C5 concept could have been a success. It cost only £399 (in the mid Eighties) and could legally be driven by a 14-year-old. It had a range of up to 20 miles (32km), and with its combination of pedal and electric power, was truly environmentally friendly. Utilizing a Hoover washing machine motor, it would probably have proven quite inexpensive to maintain if it had had the chance to prove itself.

Unfortunately, the C5 was extremely unfriendly to own and drive. Low down near the road, the non-pollution-producing C5 driver was exposed to the very worst of other people's fumes, the terror of large lorries and the mud and grime of bad weather. The electrical capabilities of the C5 were not always up to the job either, and it often refused on hills, necessitating frantic pedalling by the driver.

ABOVE
Environmentally-friendly it may have been, but the C5 was no fun. It had none of the advantages of a car, or of a scooter, or of a pedal bike, but embodied some of the disadvantages of all three.

LEFT
There was an accessory kit available for the C5, providing mud flaps, all-weather protection, a seat cushion, and a specially-made mast so that the C5 could be spotted – and avoided – in heavy traffic.

Societa Anonima Lombarda Fabbrica Automobili, Alfa, was founded in 1910 by Ugo Stella, after the liquidation of the Darracq assembly plant at Portello, of which he was the managing director. Despite a healthy following in France, Darracqs had proved unsuitable for Italian road conditions, and they also had very little in the way of either performance or brakes. From the first Alfa, the 12HP designed by Giuseppe

LEFT
Not so very many C5s were made and few survive, this one preserved for posterity in the Yorkshire Car Collection.

BELOW

There's a little of the motorbike, a touch of the car, shades of a truck, even echoes of the horse-drawn carriage – this is a hard vehicle to place. In truth, it's a five-wheeled UFO.

TOP RIGHT

The best place to have a close encounter with the UFO is Daytona Beach, in Florida, where sightings are regularly reported – though usually only encounters of the first kind.

BELOW RIGHT
The UFO is powered – and we do mean powered – by a massive seven litres of Ford engine.

ABOVE
Even though he very much approved of American production methods, Herr Porsche might well not have appreciated this VW Beetle.

RIGHT
In fact, the Beetle rear is a 'cover' for a VW-powered trike.

BELOW
A topless Beetle makes an impromptu people carrier.

Merosi, right up until the late Forties, most Alfas left the factory as a running chassis – the customer then commissioned a coachbuilder to clothe his purchase.

One of the strangest bodies of any Alfa is that built by Castagna for one Count Ricotti, an extremely wealthy gentleman from Milan who dreamed of owning something futuristic. His aluminium-bodied car was shaped like a teardrop, had portholes for side windows and traditional spoked wheels. It several respects it was ahead of its time – electric lighting, an electric horn, and a top speed of almost 87mph(140km/h). The engine was a 6-litre 4-cylinder which was produced in both normal and racing versions, the

Count's choice being the latter. The engine was mounted inside the cabin with the passengers – and unfortunately those porthole windows did not open. Count Ricotti used the car to travel to his summer villa near Lake Maggiore, and before long, the car was spotted with a large section removed from the roof. What happened to the Count's original car is unknown, but there is a replica in the fabulous Alfa-Romeo museum at Arese, and it has become known as the 'Aerodinamica'.

That the Alfa-Romeo museum exists at all is largely due to Luigi Fusi, who was head of the drawing office in the research and development department. Alfa's archives were lost during a bombing raid in 1943 which destroyed

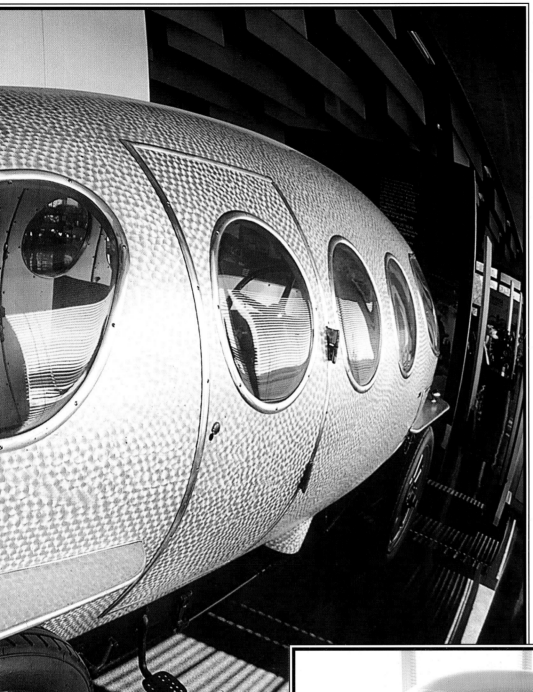

half the factory. But Fusi had kept a copy of all the designs. He was eventually given the task of tracking down examples of as many historic Alfa models as possible. Thanks to his perseverance and knowledge, a number of important Alfas were collected together, although the museum would not be housed in purpose-built premises until 1974.

LEFT
The rear of Count Ricotti's pear-drop Alfa (replica).

BELOW
The Aerodynamica has traditional spoked wheels and a cocoon-like appearance.

Chapter Four
Things 'Ain't Quite What They Seem'

I s any car quite what it seems? After all, the most we really need in a car is an engine to drive the wheels and controls to connect engine to the driver. We need somewhere to sit, and something to keep us and the weather apart. Plenty of manufacturers have gone back to basics at one time or another, often very successfully. The Citroën 2CV, the VW Beetle, the Mini, each in its own way attempted to pare down to the essentials, and keep costs to a minimum for the customer.

ABOVE

It looks like a boat, it's built like a boat – but it's a car. Andy Saunders built this ambiguous amphibious look-alike on the running gear of a 1969 Reliant Regal. The 'boat' part really is based on a boat – a Monbar 146. Everything has been incorporated inside the hull to keep the boat-shape as complete as possible.

FAR LEFT

The boat attracts lot of admiring glances – and lots of second looks – in and around the seaside town of Poole in Dorset.

LEFT

Just as you thought it was safe to come out of the water ... The boat's brilliant colour scheme and wonderful graphics say 'sun-summer-fun'. The high quality finish took many hours to achieve.

The Schwimmwagen was as impressive on land as it was on water, boasting four-wheel-drive. Maximum speed on land was 50mph (80km/h), and in the water 6mph (10km/h). There were two fuel tanks, and a pressure system for lubricating the front axle – necessary when in the water.

Making a production car 'not what it seems' is a job for both the stylists and the marketing gurus. While some classic shapes – that of the Porsche 911 for example – are enduring and beyond fashion, other style phases come and go. Fearsomely wedge-shaped or round

and cuddly, its all down to what we want to buy, and what the manufacturers can persuade us we want to buy. Making a one-off is different, of course. The only limits are imagination, time and money.

The year was 1939. Ferdinand

RIGHT
The earliest Schwimmwagen came with the 984cc engine, but later came with a version of the 1131cc unit, bored out to give the minimum power that military regulations demanded. The final version, thought by many to be the best of all, had a shorter wheelbase and lower weight.

BELOW
The exhaust outlet and air intakes had to be fitted well above 'high water' level. The indentation in the engine cover accommodates the propeller when in the raised position.

Porsche had only been able to partially realize his long-held dream of building a small car. It was a project that he had been trying to get off the ground for many years – but each time he thought he had a buyer or an interested backer, something happened to scupper the

LEFT
One advantage that the Orange had over some other promotional vehicles is that passengers could be carried with relative ease.

RIGHT
The interior theme is relentlessly orange, with segmented roof, sides, seats, and orange tinted windows to extend the effect to the rest of the world.

plan. Design and testing of Hitler's KdF-Wagen (Strength through Joy Car) had been fraught with difficulty and restrictions, but it had seemed to Porsche that his dream was in with a chance, and of course he had no way of knowing what the future would hold.

So now there was a war, and Porsche was receiving instructions to design a military vehicle based on the Volkswagen. The VW as it stood would not do – it was nowhere near rugged enough for the job in hand – so a major redesign was the only option. Porsche decided that he needed an engine of at least 1134cc instead of the original 995cc even though this meant redesigns for most of the other components too – there was no alternative. The new vehicle would have to carry considerable weights in unfavourable conditions, so it needed to be tough. Porsche came up with a reinforced chassis and gutsier suspension – in short, something that would do the job. There was no need to get bogged down on the subtler points of good looks either – this was a workhorse, not a styling exercise.

The prototypes of the new vehicle – which became known as the

'Top Cat' – the car that Bill Carter built around a disassembled Jaguar XJ12 is used for promotional purposes by Ordnance Survey and Bosch. Another car that gets a lot of attention at events – and even more when Bill takes it down to the shops!

Kubelwagen (Kubel = tub!) were put through their paces and performed well under test, much to the amazement of the authorities. Military chiefs discovered that the Kubel did just as well if not better than their favourite four-wheel-drives. They were also

lighter and far easier to handle. So the go-ahead was given for the Kubel to start production.

The new factory for the Volkswagen at Wolfsburg was as yet unfinished, so bodies for the Kubelwagen were manufactured by Ambi-Budd in Berlin

during the course of the war.

Several different versions of the Kubelwagen were made for special purposes. There was a half-track for particularly difficult terrain, dummy tanks for training, and test cars for a four-wheel-drive version. And there was the Schwimmwagen, a Volkswagen which could, indeed, swim. The Schwimmwagen was amphibious, equally at home on land as in the water. Obviously there were no doors – to get in you just clambered over the side, but there was a folding canvas hood to offer some weather protection. The 'boat's' propeller was driven directly by the rear-mounted engine and could be disengaged and raised with a detachable rod when the 'car' was in land-mode. Over 14,000 Schwimmwagens were manufactured in all. In addition to doing a good job, they were a popular drive. When Allied troops had the opportunity to try some at the end of the war, they found them an endless source of enjoyment, especially when changing from land to water – most impressive when demonstrated to an audience who don't know what's coming!

The Schwimmwagen does not look like a VW Beetle, and the Orange does not look like a Mini – and here at the point of non-similar similarity, the similarity ends! For the Orange is fun, it raises a smile wherever it goes, it is sunny, round and dimply, and it is very, very orange. The Oranges, for there are in fact four of them, have been around since the early Seventies. They were commissioned by the Outspan fruit company as an advertising and promotional gimmick, a job at which they excelled. They could often be seen at county shows and country fairs, as well as trade events and business exhibitions. During the Eighties, Outspan restricted their promotional activities because they found reaction to their South African origins was not always favourable, and the Oranges

and transported to Wolfsburg to be assembled. The new Kubelwagen proved itself rapidly. It was a tough and practical vehicle, performing equally well in the heat and sand of North Africa as the bitter snows of Russia. One innovation was an

ingenious rear lighting system to help following vehicles judge distance. Several of the bulbs were placed behind varying thicknesses of green glass; the nearer to the Kubelwagen you were, the more lights were visible. In total, 50,000 Kubelwagens were made

were not often seen. Three of the
Oranges are still used today for their
original purpose by Capespan – the
company formed when Outspan
merged with Cape – although the fourth
example now resides in the Motor
Museum at Beaulieu.

The Orange is based on the 1000cc
Mini, fitted with a three-speed
automatic gearbox. Both track and
wheelbase are 48ins (1.21m), giving a
squarely firm base for the spherical
bodywork which is made of fibreglass
and dimpled just like a real orange.
Inside the Orange, the theme continues,
the segments of the padded roof coming
together at a point above the
windscreen, just where the 'stalk' is on
the outside. Driving it is quite an
experience – it takes some getting used
to; the two pedals are not difficult to
reach, although our man, both tall and
quite large of foot and girth found the
driving position uncomfortable, and
had to duck to see out of the
windscreen – which incidentally is the
only window not orange-tinted. In all,
he didn't count himself totally 'in
control of the vehicle' for the first few
minutes, but enjoyed it once it felt
safer! There is no criticism here of the
Orange of course – it was not designed
for long distance luxury or grand
touring!

There have been many promotional
vehicles in the shape of the product –
bottles of champagne and beer barrels,
ice creams and cakes, bananas and
eggs. But perhaps because the Orange is
the car, rather than just being an add-
on to a more conventional road vehicle,
it has always been very popular
everywhere it goes.

If your main line of business is the
importing of citrus fruit, your choice of
body-style for the promotional

RIGHT
'G-whizz' – another car by Bill Carter. Not a
car that is easily ignored

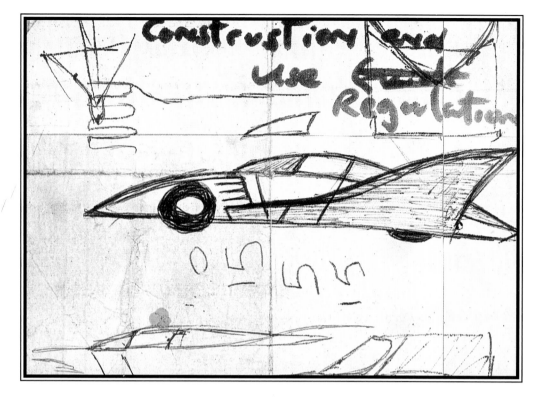

has a feel for how a motor car should fit together, which stems from many years of experience and a good deal of natural talent.

'Top Cat' started life on Bill's garage floor as a series of parts from a 1974 Jaguar XJ12. When the car had formed itself in his mind from this starting point, Bill constructed the chassis. He found a way of raising and lowering the front suspension to give the low-riding effect that he was after without the possibility of damage when the car was being driven about – for Bill does like his cars to be driven rather than put on a transporter. The 5.3-litre engine from the Jaguar was fitted, with the addition of six Weber carbs and electronic ignition.

TOP
Andy Saunder's sketch for a supercar ...

ABOVE
You wouldn't expect to find a normal, boring interior in this car, would you?

vehicle largely suggests itself. If on the other hand your product is top-quality maps and mapping, the possibilities are endless. Fortunately for Ordnance Survey, they already employed the services of Bill Carter, graphic designer and builder of strange and interesting motor cars. But Bill doesn't just make cars that look good, he makes sure they work well and reliably and are comfortable and fun to drive, too. He

RIGHT and BELOW
This car is based upon a Citroën CX; all
body parts are in steel, and were completely
redesigned and painted by Andy himself.

For the body, Bill took an unusual approach. Many builders of one-off cars must have searched the scrap yards and secondhand ads for suitable parts, but through a friend Bill managed to get hold of the ultimate – a scrapped canopy from an R.A.F. Tornado. With this positioned, Bill used boat-building techniques to shape the remainder of the body, constructing wooden profiles from which moulds were made. The final fibreglass panels could then be produced. Bill's aim was to use curved shapes wherever possible for a streamlined and highly stylized look. He sprayed the car himself, finishing the effect with many layers of clear lacquer. The headlamps come courtesy of the Vauxhall Calibra, the rear light clusters being Bill's own design and make.

You might be forgiven for expecting the inside of the Top Cat to be spartan and functional, but you would be wrong. The car has power steering, air conditioning, extremely comfortable seats, and is finished to a high standard. And because of the job of work the car is called upon to do, it proudly promotes its Bosch computerized navigation system. Top Cat is low, over 6ft (1.8m) wide and, at 23ft (7m) long, is certainly eye-catching. Bill drives the car around town quite successfully – it always turns heads – but when let loose Top Cat can reach 160mph (257km/h). Fuel consumption is in the region of 10mpg (3 ltr/km).

Although the Top Cat took Bill 19 months to build from start to finish, this is not a one-off dream fulfilled. He has also built at least half a dozen other cars, including the G-Whizz, a two-seater which took almost two years to complete. The car, which uses the chassis of a Daimler saloon, Jaguar XJ12 engine and another jet canopy, this

ABOVE
Although the Scorpion is 'only' a three-wheeler, it can match with pride the stability and performance of many a sports car. Unlike many bike-based cars, such as the Messerschmitt, the driver and passenger sit side-by-side in the Scorpion.

ABOVE

The Scorpion is not too expensive to run. It can do 50mpg (18 ltr/km) and qualifies as a motorcycle and sidecar combination, which means a saving on road tax. It can be driven by anyone with a motorbike licence.

RIGHT

The Scorpion is bought in kit form, the purchaser carrying out whatever proportion of the finishing work he wishes, from building the whole thing right down to just fitting the steering wheel.

time from a Hawk, uses 20-gallon (90-ltr) metal beer kegs as fuel tanks. Its top speed is slightly lower than Top Cat at 150mph (241km/h), but it does manage 12mpg (4.2 ltr/km)! This car turns heads too, and has been described as looking like an earthbound plane. It is 21ft (6.4m) long, and has moving tail-fins, a state-of-the-art CB radio, and an on-board video camera which relays pictures of the road behind to a monitor in the cockpit. Like all Bill's projects, G-Whizz is taxed, with MOT and insurance, and is in every respect a completely road-legal motor car.

The story of the Grinnall Scorpion began in 1991, when Mark Grinnall began the research and development programme for a new type of vehicle.

Grinnall Cars had been trading since the early Eighties, mainly building and restoring Triumph TR7s and TR8s. In 1992, freelance car designer Steve Harper was commissioned to style the new creation. Steve had previously been involved in, among other things, the Escort Cosworth projects. The first preproduction Scorpion model got its first journalistic airing in the June edition of *Autocar*. Production began in earnest the following year, with the Scorpion selling well from the start both in the U.K. and European markets.

Performance is staggering. Fitted with the K1100 16-valve engine, the Scorpion is capable of 0-60mph (0-100km) in 5 seconds, and a top speed of 130mph (209km/h). This engine

produces 100 bhp, while the K1000 8-valve produces 90bhp. The 16-valve units are all fitted with BMW's Para-Lever rear suspension system. The cars are available either in kit form or ready assembled. Usually they will be fitted with new BMW parts, but low-mileage second-hand engines can be fitted too, which is obviously much cheaper for the customer. Despite its performance, the Scorpion can manage 50mpg (18 ltr/km), and qualifies as a motorcycle in the U.K.

As well as many fine vintage and classic cars old and new, some of which can be seen elsewhere in this book, the Yorkshire Car Collection also boasts a unique Ferrari. This is one of several world-famous cars used to pace the PPG

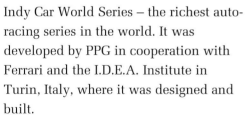

LEFT
Ferrari styling ... magnificent!

ABOVE
The two banks of yellow lamps flash at random when the car is pacing – very easy to spot, even if you miss the bright red Ferrari.

BELOW
Naturally, the interior is especially kitted out for the job in hand, communication being a prime priority.

Indy Car World Series – the richest auto-racing series in the world. It was developed by PPG in cooperation with Ferrari and the I.D.E.A. Institute in Turin, Italy, where it was designed and built.

This car was the first European car to be used as an Indy pace car. It was designed and engineered by Ferrari, and powered by the prototype Testarossa engine. It was built in 1988 and in use until the end of the 1993 season, being used as the lead car at the Laguna Beach circuit. This is a true concept car – the only one of its kind to be built. The pace car team is interesting, comprising 13 well-known women racing drivers, all of whom have earned recognition in their own branch of the sport.

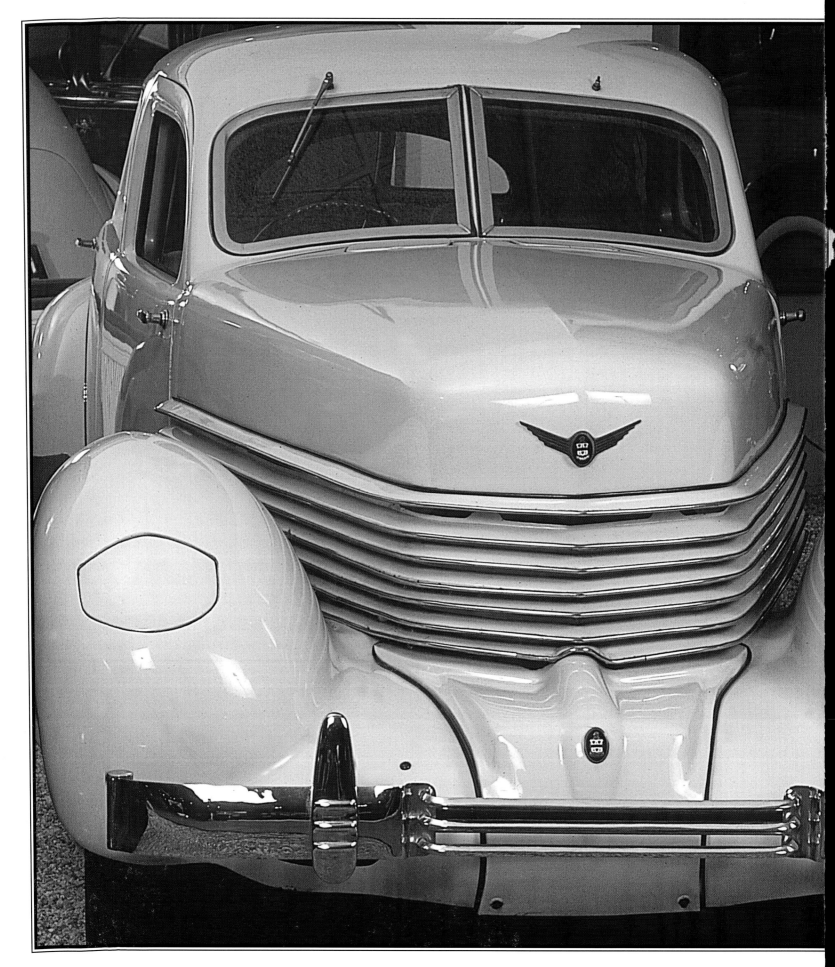

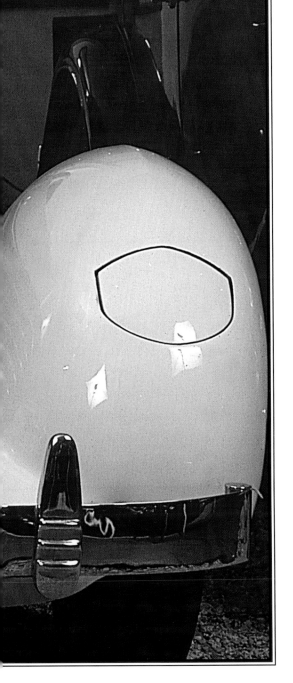

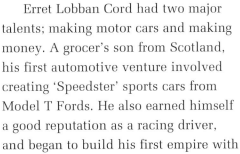

Erret Lobban Cord had two major talents; making motor cars and making money. A grocer's son from Scotland, his first automotive venture involved creating 'Speedster' sports cars from Model T Fords. He also earned himself a good reputation as a racing driver, and began to build his first empire with the purchase of a garage and filling station. He then invested the money he made in a trucking company, but business failed, and Cord moved to Chicago to start afresh.

Within a very few years, Cord was starting to build up his fortune again. He bought out several companies,

including the automobile business that the Duesenberg brothers had built up. But Cord had long planned to build a car which would cary his own name, a dream which he first realized in 1929 with his first L-29 Cabriolet.

The Rotrax is an unusual recreational vehicle, similar to the beach buggies, but it is a lot more practical, as it is both safer and stronger. It is also faster, and therefore more fun, too. But the Rotrax can also work for its living. It is designed to be able to tow heavy boats, and can also be fitted with roof bars and to take surfboards, sails and so on. The four-wheel-drive model has serious off-road capabilities, while the two-wheel-drive version is intended primarily for road use.

Rotrax was created by Dennis Adams, the designer of the Marcos 1800 and Mantula convertible. Adams has also been responsible for designing special-bodied Land Rovers and Range Rovers, mainly for customers in the Middle East. Rotrax is based on the Ford Cortina MK 3,4 or 5. These old cars sell cheaply, and although many of the body shells have rusted away, the mechanical parts often survive in good condition, and the gearboxes in particular are well thought of. Parts for the cars are cheap and plentiful, too. For extra power, the Ford V6 engine can be fitted. Rotrax comes in kit form and is reckoned to be quite easy to construct in around 75-100 hours for someone with basic knowledge and standard tools.

LEFT
The Rotrax – looking like a life-sized Tonka toy – is fun to drive and turns heads wherever it goes.

Chapter Five
Every Picture Tells a Story

ABOVE
The car was styled to give the look of an authentic 1960s American showcar: heavily customized detail and accentuating graphics, wire wheels, white-wall tyres. Everything has been geared to capturing the spirit of America in the early Sixties.

LEFT
This outrageous machine was created by Andy Saunders from a poor unsuspecting Volvo Amazon two-door saloon, originally made in 1961. Any resemblance between the car today and how it looked then is either coincidental or a product of a vivid imagination.

ABOVE

A previous incarnation of the very same Volvo. No less loud, this version had embroidered pictures on the seats. So often with 'one-off productions' such as this, endless care and attention is lavished on getting just the right effect, with period decoration down to the very last detail. Although the cars are very often the brain child of one person who masterminds them from conception to completion, the finished effect frequently owes much to a team – spouses, parents, children, siblings, friends and colleagues – anyone with a particular skill can and will be commandeered into the team for the duration.

LEFT

Candy-striped interior suggests summer days. Chromework and white fixtures and fittings complete the picture. Everything is finished with great attention to detail – for example, the colour-coordinated steering wheel boss.

ABOVE

The interior of this Porsche special is silver. Silver leather covers every surface, even the gearstick and handbreak handle. Unfortunately, the businessman couldn't pay for the car when it was ready; this is not a car that everyone would fancy, so it wasn't easy to sell.

RIGHT

The Porsche 928 is a fine-looking motor car in its natural state. This special was ordered by a Japanese businessman who wanted something rather different. The gullwing doors, the special paint, the accent on silver – the man had seriously metallic tastes.

LEFT
This Mini is another car built by Andy
Saunders, aided and abetted by Scott Lloyd.
The 'slit' windows and reshaping combine
to give the car an extremely new-style
Japanese concept-car look.

ABOVE
The original Mini was of 1963 vintage. Its
roof was removed, and approximately 9
inches chopped from the height. The
replacement roof was from a Vauxhall
Astra van.

BELOW
Inside the Mini; the seats are comfortable
and the interior sympathetically finished –
it pays not to be too tall, though.

LEFT

This particular Nash was brought to England for the Yorkshire Car Collection. In the boot when it arrived were the optional extras of the day; mattresses to cover the seats which could be made to fully recline...

LEFT

Charles W. Nash started his company in 1917 in Kenosha, Wisconsin, having formerly been President of General Motors. He produced only 6-cylinder cars between 1945 and 1954, 150,000 of them Ambassador models like this one. The Ambassador was a much improved, restyled successor to the Airflyte. The bodywork at front-wheel level was curiously skirted, a Nash trade-mark that only served to give the car a huge and extremely unpopular turning circle.

BELOW

...and mosquito screens for the windows.

RIGHT

The car's suspension lifts by 12 inches, and not just at the rear. The car can be made to dance about and, most impressively of all, this can be done by remote control – guaranteed to provide hours of innocent fun making people jump out of their skins in car parks!

104

LEFT
These trikes are mean machines.

LEFT
Startrike is fitted with a V8 engine with twin superchargers.

RIGHT
Startrike – one of the beautifully decorated machines at Daytona Beach.

BELOW
Speed is not the only consideration at the annual Daytona get-together; the trikes embody a lifestyle all of their own.

ABOVE
A man on a mission; owner Trooper
Trudeau sets out.

RIGHT
An unusual vehicle, constructed from a
1936 Harley-Davidson sidecar and a 1941
motorbike from the same stable. The whole
was fashioned by Trooper Trudeau,
pictured here, and is capable of over
100mph(160km/h).

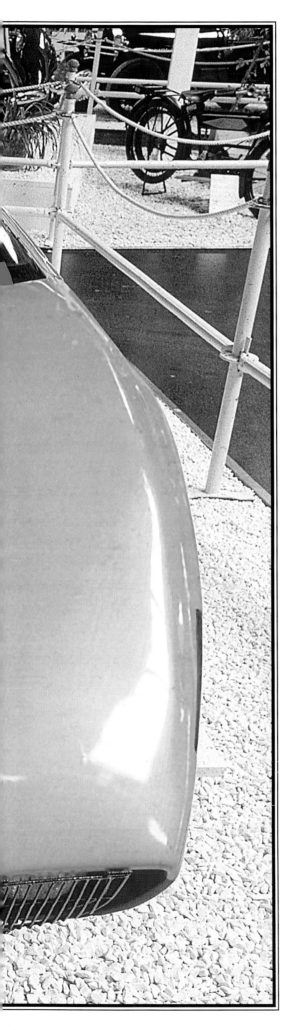

LEFT
This diesel-powered Mercedes is to be
found in the Mercedes-Benz museum at
Unterturkheim. The C111 was built in the
early Seventies as an experimental vehicle;
many of the lessons learned from it
influenced Mercedes production cars, but it
was also an amazing car in its own right,
breaking several speed records.

ABOVE
This one-off Beetle at a Custom show in
Germany is about to take flight. With its
gull-wings it possibly thinks it is a
Mercedes, or Porsche perhaps?

INDEX

Pages in italics refer to illustrations